KS2 Skills Practice
ENGLISH
Learning Adventures

Anne Loadman

Introduction

About this book

This book provides lots of practice in developing the essential skills your child will need during the literacy hour at school and when preparing for the National Tests at the end of KS2. In particular, it concentrates on making your child's writing clear and interesting and gives tips on how to plan and structure writing tasks. So why not join The Gang to find out more about English and what fun it can be!

How to use this book

Think about the best time for using this book. It might be easier at a weekend or early in the evening. Most of all, pick a quiet time when your child is eager to learn and not too tired. Find a suitable place where he or she can work comfortably without being disturbed, then make a start on one of the activities.

Your child may prefer to work through the book page by page, or alternatively you could suggest activities that you feel will be more useful. Whichever approach you adopt, try to make it an enjoyable and positive experience for your child. Discuss the activities together and give lots of praise and encouragement along the way. Words highlighted in red throughout the book can be found in the Glossary on page 44 and all the answers are at the back of the book for quick and easy checking! Your child will need paper for some of the activities.

How you can help

- Encourage your child to read a range of reading material, for example: novels, as well as poetry, non-fiction, instructions, plays, newspapers and magazines (say for 10 to 15 minutes a day) and then to discuss what he or she has read with you, asking questions about the content of the text and their opinions about it.
- Remember little and often is best! Children's brains can only take so much, it's best to stop before they get bored and grumpy.
- You can help your child by reading questions, testing knowledge of facts, marking answers and discussing topics that your child finds difficult.
- Use the *Spark Island KS2 National Tests English* for some more exciting activities, or log on to the Spark Island website (www.sparkisland.com) for your child to take part in some interactive fun.
- Most of all encourage your child, praise his or her efforts and use the gold stickers to reward good work.

Contents

Introduction	2
Starting and ending sentences	4
Connectives and conjunctions	6
Commas and colons	8
Clauses	10
Semi-colons and brackets	12
Adjectives	14
Similes and metaphors	16
Adverbs	18
Direct speech	20
Standard English and agreeing tenses	22
Apostrophes	24
Planning stories	26
Beginning and ending stories	28
Descriptions	30
Writing in paragraphs	32
Letter writing	34
Persuasive writing	36
Play scripts and interviews	38
Writing instructions	40
Journalistic and leaflet writing	42
Glossary	44
Answers	45

Starting and ending sentences

Remember to use capital letters and full stops in your own writing.

Sentences or statements start with a capital letter and end with a full stop. Capital letters are used:
- at the beginning of people's names
- for place names and titles
- for days of the week and months of the year.

1 Milo is sad because the mischievous Malvos have taken all the capital letters and full stops from his diary. Circle all the letters that should be capitals and replace all the full stops.

monday 14th october

today has been very good i played a trick on zeb by hiding his favourite book he was looking all over for it nina tried to help him they even went to the library in sparkopolis and searched every part of sparkley square i had to tell them the truth eventually and they were mad zeb even thought the xybok had eaten it by mistake, thinking its red cover was a giant raspberry i laughed for ages now i need to think up a new trick for tuesday

Nouns, or naming words, that need capital letters are called **proper nouns**. Some examples of proper nouns are people's names, place names, days of the week and months of the year.

Nouns that don't need a capital letter are called **common** nouns, e.g. table, chair, boy.

2 Sort the words on the right into proper nouns and common nouns and put them in the correct columns.

Proper nouns	Common nouns

Tuesday Brighton Fifi cat school hedge England Strat book raspberry fork River Thames

Write ten more examples in two columns on a separate piece of paper.

- Ordinary sentences, or statements, need a full stop.
  Sparkopolis is the capital of Spark Island.
- Always end questions with a question mark.
  Do you live in Blackspark Road?
- Commands and exclamations need an exclamation mark.
  Stop! Ouch!

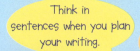
Think in sentences when you plan your writing.

Always check your punctuation when you have finished your work.

3 Find the three different kinds of sentences below and punctuate them. Add a full stop, question mark or exclamation mark to each one.

(a) Are you coming swimming today___
(b) Stop that now___
(c) Sparkopolis is a big city___
(d) Statements must end with a full stop___
(e) Are you going to eat all that cake yourself___
(f) Leave him alone___
(g) Dotty is a dreamer, isn't she___
(h) It was absolutely fantastic___
(i) Have you got any homework tonight___
(j) I wonder how many sentences I've got right___

Remember
- Read sentences carefully to find their meaning.
- Look for clues like question marks and exclamation marks.
- Use question marks and exclamation marks in your own writing.

Question marks and exclamation marks are often used in interviews.

4 Read the interview below and count how many question marks and exclamation marks have been used.

Zeb: Good evening, Strat. I would like to start by asking you what brings you to Spark Island?

Strat: Well, I was saved from Dame Drusilla's orphanage. I was so glad to get out of there!

Zeb: What do you like about living here?

Strat: Spark Island is a very interesting place. There's always something new to do. Yesterday I found a secret cave that was covered in stalactites and stalagmites!

Zeb: Really? How amazing! But don't you have to be careful when you're exploring?

Strat: Yes, I never go alone and I always tell someone where I'm going.

How many of each did you count?   Try writing your own interview.

Connectives and conjunctions

Connectives and conjunctions are joining words. They are useful for making two short sentences into a longer, more complex one. Here are some common connectives:

| so | but | and | then | because |

If you are not sure what any words mean, look them up in a dictionary.

1 Look at these short sentences. Join them together using the connectives above. The first one has been done for you.

> Milo had no money left. He could not buy sweets.
> Milo had no money left so he could not buy sweets.
>
> (a) Nina was miserable. Nobody wanted to go out.
> _____
>
> (b) Strat is popular. He is the leader of the Gang.
> _____
>
> (c) Dotty went to the library. She went to Spark Park.
> _____
>
> (d) Zeb likes reference books. He likes to collect facts.
> _____

Here are some more connectives:
therefore
consequently
however
although

Remember
When you use **consequently** or **therefore** to join two sentences, you can use a semi-colon just before the second part of the sentence.
We had no milk left; consequently we couldn't eat our cereal.

2 On a separate piece of paper, write some pairs of sentences and then use a connective to join each pair together to make a longer sentence.

3 Put the missing connectives into these sentences using the connectives in the blue box above.

> (a) Spark Island is a fun place; _____ people like living there.
> (b) Crombies are very studious people, _____ they are friendly.
> (c) Milo can be very sensible, _____ he often sulks.
> (d) Crombies are very quiet, _____ Spironauts are definitely not!

6

Sometimes connectives are used so that sentences follow on easily from one to another.
We are going to play football now. Later, we may go to the beach.
In this sentence, the word **later** is used as a connective.
There are lots of connectives to do with time. Here are some of them.

a few years later   in less than a second   afterwards   soon after   meanwhile

4 Use one of the connectives above to link the following sentences.

(a) The Elders fired up the magic sparkler machine. _____ bright coloured sparks were spinning out from the funnel.

(b) Dotty went off to look for Strat's lost trainer. _____ he had found another pair he could wear.

(c) The Elders had a marvellous idea to build a huge, new library. _____ it was finished.

(d) The Malvos are very crafty. _____ they can trick people into giving them what they want.

Connective words are often used in recipes and instructions to show the order in which to do things.
First, take the eggs, **then** …… **Lastly** …… .

5 Complete this recipe for a cheese sandwich using suitable connective words from the box.

finally   then   after that   secondly   first

(a) _____ take two slices of bread and spread with butter or margarine.

(b) _____ slice or grate the cheese onto a small plate.

(c) _____ arrange the cheese on the bread.

(d) _____ add pickle or mayonnaise or any topping of your choice.

(e) _____ put the other slice of bread on top and cut into halves or quarters.

Serve with salad and a cold glass of lemonade or milk. Enjoy!

Commas and colons

Commas are useful, especially when you're writing lists.

Commas separate items in a list, to stop you getting confused.
The rule is: use a comma after every item in a list, but, when you get to the end, separate the last two items with the word **and**.

*In my pocket were coins, string, bubble gum, a pen **and** my key.*

1 Put commas into these sentences.

(a) The Elders needed Lixir unicycles raspberries and books.
(b) Nina tidied out her bag. She found sweets a book a map of Sparkopolis a pencil and a button from her coat.
(c) To get to the park go straight along Blackmore Road turn right then left and cross over by the library.
(d) To make the model you will need card glue thin string pens scissors a paper fastener and a lot of patience!
(e) The library is open on Monday Tuesday Wednesday and Friday.

2 Now write some lists which would follow on from these sentence starts. Don't forget to add commas and end with a full stop.

(a) In Strat's hand were _____

(b) In the newspaper there were articles about _____

(c) On the table you could see _____

(d) Milo had been collecting things in his cap. He had _____

3 Look around the house and see if you can find some interesting collections that you could write as lists, e.g. the contents of your bedside cabinet drawer or your school bag, collections of models, stickers or CDs.

Colons which look like this : can also be used to introduce lists.

> Five things to remember when crossing a road: choose a safe place, stop, look, listen and keep looking and listening as you cross.

4 Make your own lists using the ideas below.

(a) Five things you might find in a magician's pocket: _____

(b) Four things you might find in a footballer's sports bag: _____

(c) Six things you might find in a pop star's pocket: _____

Colons can also be used to separate two parts of a sentence, when they are connected but you want to have a pause. You should only use a colon when the first part of each sentence could stand by itself.

> There was only one thing left to ask: who had won the competition.

5 Add a colon to each of these sentence starts and think of your own way of finishing them.

(a) He had an idea _____

(b) She knew what she had to do _____

(c) The thought came to him _____

(d) It seemed like the only answer _____

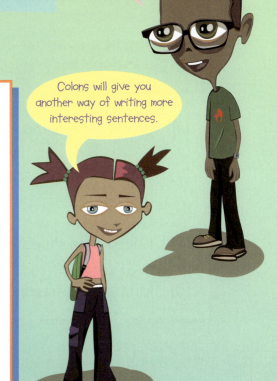

Colons can make your writing look and sound grown-up if you use them correctly.

Colons will give you another way of writing more interesting sentences.

Clauses

- A **clause** is a group of words, which includes a verb and makes sense by itself.
  I am happy. We opened the door.

- The most important words in a sentence are called the **main clause**. These give the most important information.

- Clauses can be added together to make longer, more complicated sentences and are separated by a comma.

- Clauses are often joined by connectives such as **who**, **where**, **although** etc.
  *We went to Spark Park, **where** we saw many strange creatures.*

  In this sentence the word **where** is the connective word.

1 Use a comma to separate the two clauses in each of the following sentences and circle the connective.

  (a) Strat was bored but he knew that an adventure wasn't far away.

  (b) Everyone laughed although poor Milo got soaking wet.

  (c) The diver explored the sea bed even though there were sharks nearby.

  (d) You can't go out unless you tidy your room first.

Here are some more connectives:
especially since
unless
because
while
even though

2 Choose the best connective to join each of following two clauses together.

  (a) Nina kept smiling, _____ her ankle was hurting a lot.

  (b) The book was fascinating, _____ it had been written hundreds of years ago.

  (c) I need new shoes, _____ these are too small.

  (d) Milo played baseball, _____ Dotty practised on her rollerblades.

3 Now try and make up some more sentences of your own, separate them with a comma and join them with a connective.

Sometimes, instead of the clauses in a sentence being separate, the main clause is wrapped around another clause; with a bit at the beginning and a bit at the end.

Strat, **who was the leader of the Gang**, was happy.

The main clause is Strat was happy; the secondary, or subordinate, clause: who was the leader of the Gang has been inserted in the middle of the main clause to give more information.

Commas are used before and after the secondary clause to separate it from the main clause.

4 Add commas to separate the main clause from the secondary (subordinate) clause.

(a) Nina who is a friendly girl rarely loses her temper.
(b) While visiting the zoo Milo who was the youngest of the Gang got lost.
(c) Sparkopolis which is a large city was designed by the Elders.
(d) Strat hoped as he unlocked the box he would find the treasure.

5 Here are two sets of clauses. Make a complex sentence by wrapping the main clause around the subordinate clause.

Don't forget your commas.

Main clause	Subordinate clause
She got up and left.	because she was tired

She got up, because she was tired, and left.

Strat had a sore eye.	after being hit by the ball
Nina jumped over the hedge.	because she was being chased by a bull
Milo can be mischievous.	who is the youngest

You can add more clauses together to make longer sentences.

The dog ran away, with the ball in his mouth, even though he was being chased by everyone.

Remember to separate the clauses with commas and end with a full stop.

Practise writing clauses until you can use them easily.

Semi-colons and brackets

Semi-colons are used in sentences where a pause is needed but where the two parts of the sentence are connected.

Gary was a good singer; Kevin croaked like a frog.

1 Make sentences using a sentence start and a sentence ending from the columns below. Punctuate each one with a semi-colon.

Starts	Endings
It was nearly midnight	I think you prefer blue.
Your book looks interesting	I keep my photos in this box.
I keep my stickers in this album	everyone had gone to bed.
My favourite colour is red	mine is a mystery story.

(a) _____

(b) _____

(c) _____

(d) _____

2 Here is a paragraph from a story start. Put in the semi-colons where they are needed to make the paragraph read better.

You need 5 semi-colons.

It was a winter's night cold and dark. In the trees, owls hooted overhead on the forest floor, small creatures scampered through leaves. Strat was glad of his torch it had been a present from Nina. Everywhere he moved, eyes seemed to follow him huge, staring eyes. Strat shivered and pulled his coat around him. He couldn't give up now he had to go on.

You can use brackets to go round words that nobody is supposed to hear, or which are an extra part of a sentence.

'You look lovely in that hat, Dotty,' lied Milo (actually he thought it looked like a plant pot).

Or The picture (shown on page 1) was drawn by Stefi, the international artist.

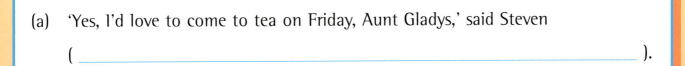

Brackets are fun to use.

3 Fill in the brackets in the following sentences with words that tell us what the characters are thinking or doing.

(a) 'Yes, I'd love to come to tea on Friday, Aunt Gladys,' said Steven (_____).

(b) Milo (who was _____ as usual) pretended he had done his homework.

(c) The footballer shouted for a penalty (although _____) and the referee blew the whistle.

Remember
- Look for brackets in books you read and see how they are used.
- Add brackets to your own writing, especially when one character is saying something that he or she doesn't want the other characters to know.

4 Read the sentences below and put brackets round the parts that you think are extra to the meaning.

(a) The Elders although wise were incredibly forgetful.
(b) The Phliplids were rebuilding their so far invisible spaceship.
(c) The Malvos denied upsetting the Crombies as they always do but the Crombies were convinced of their guilt.
(d) Milo had borrowed Zeb's encyclopedia without permission and now had raspberry jam all over the cover.

Adjectives

A thesaurus is a good place to find a range of adjectives.

Adjectives are describing words used to describe nouns. Choosing good adjectives can make your writing come to life.

Some adjectives are to do with size.
These words are similar in meaning to 'small'.

tiny   miniscule   microscopic   undersized   short

These words are similar in meaning to 'big'.

large   enormous   gigantic   mountainous   oversized   tall

1 Choose suitable adjectives from the box above and put them into the sentences below.

(a) The _____ mouse ran across the kitchen floor.

(b) It was the most _____ sandcastle I had ever built.

(c) The _____ flea jumped onto the _____ dog.

(d) The _____ tree towered above them.

2 Adjectives can also describe the colour, shape, feel, smell and taste of an object. Underline the adjectives in the following sentences.

(a) I couldn't wait to eat the sweet orange.
(b) The old castle walls felt rough and damp.
(c) The stormy sea sent waves of salty water over the harbour.
(d) The beautiful scent of flowers filled the small room.

When you use more than one adjective in a sentence, separate them with a comma, as you would in a list.

The boy kicked the small, round, leather football straight into the goal.

3 Add three adjectives to each of these sentences to make them more interesting.

Remember, don't put a comma after the last adjective you use.

(a) It was a _____ , _____ , _____ night.

(b) I was given a _____ , _____ , _____ book.

(c) The door of the _____ , _____ , _____ castle creaked open.

To add even more detail to your descriptions you can add a 'qualifying' word to the beginning of your description.
Words like: **really**, **extremely** and **very** can be used for descriptive effect.

The large, golden sun was **extremely** bright that day.

The use of **extremely** tells us that on this day the sun was even brighter than usual.

These are some of the words you can add to adjectives.

| really | awfully | amazingly | wonderfully | extremely |
| very | frighteningly | beautifully | horribly | incredibly |

4 Add one of the words from the box above to these sentences to make the adjectives even more interesting.

(a) She was a _____ talented girl.

(b) He was a _____ skilful player.

(c) It was a _____ enormous mountain.

(d) I had never seen such a _____ scary film.

Adjectives are often used for comparing objects. Adding **-er** or **-est** to the end of adjectives makes them comparative.

This apple is red; that one is **redder**, but that big apple is the **reddest**.

For longer words, **more** and **most** or **less** and **least** are used in front of the adjectives to make them comparisons.

The second film was **more** exciting than the first, but the latest one is the **most** exciting.

5 Underline the adjectives, including the comparative words used, in these sentences.

(a) He was the most awful footballer I have ever seen.

(b) She was the least shy person in the room.

(c) She was the loudest singer in the group.

(d) He had one older brother and two younger sisters.

Remember
When you want to compare good or bad, the rule is:
good, better, best – bad, worse, worst.
Don't get caught out!

Similes and metaphors

Another way to describe things is to use a simile.

A simile is a phrase saying something is like something else, or as _____ as something else.

   The moon was as bright as a silver coin.
       The wind blew round the man like an icy cloak.

Similes are good to use in character descriptions or to set the scene or atmosphere in a story.

1 Choose a different simile to add to each sentence of this story scene setter.

   like dragon's teeth   as big as an elephant   as timidly as mice

   a sound like thunder   like a grey giant   like washing on a line

The castle stood _____ on the top of the hill.
Its battlements were _____ and flags flew
from each turret _____. The huge, strong door
loomed up in front of us _____ and we
knocked _____. From behind the door,
_____ echoed across the flagstones.
Someone was approaching!

2 Use similes to write a descriptive poem about anything you like. Here's one about the sea to give you an idea.

> The sea lay as flat as glass,
> Bright as a mirror in the sun's light.
> And deep beneath, like tiny darts
> Small fish swimming, left and right.

16

Metaphors say that something **is** something else.

The sun is a huge orange in a big, blue bowl.

We know that the sun is a star, not an orange, but it is effective sometimes to describe something in this way.

Metaphors can be particularly useful when writing poetry:

Snow is icing draped over a wedding cake,
It is a feather pillow bursting in Heaven.
Snow is magic dust left by a million wizards,
Snow is a blanket covering the tired earth.

Metaphors are another way of describing something or someone.

I love poetry. I can use the pictures in my head to describe things to another reader so they can share my ideas.

3 Think of something like snow, or the sun, or an emotion like anger, or fear, and write a metaphor poem about it. It doesn't have to be very long and it doesn't have to rhyme!

Practise using similes and metaphors – they're fun.

Remember
- Similes say something is **as** ___ **as** something else or **like** something.
- Metaphors say something **is** something else.

Adverbs

Verbs are doing and being words.
Adverbs tell us more about a verb. They tell us how somebody does something.
   The mountain climber **clambered carefully** up the rock face.
In this sentence, clambered is the verb (it tells us what the mountain climber did) and carefully is the adverb (it tells us how he did it).

1 In these sentences, pick a suitable adverb to go with each verb. Make sure your sentences make sense!

   happily   excitedly   carefully   silently   quickly

(a) Strat crept _____ through the pirates' caves.

(b) Milo dreamed _____ of getting a new baseball cap.

(c) Zeb read the instructions _____ before trying the experiment.

(d) Dotty rode her bike _____ down the road.

(e) Nina spoke _____ about her adventures.

Did you notice that all of the adverbs so far have ended in -ly?

An easy way to turn most adjectives into adverbs is to add **-ly**, sad becomes sadly.
Or take off the -y and add **-ily** if the adjective ends in a -y, happy becomes happily.

2 Change these adjectives into adverbs by using either -ly or -ily.

   bad _____   merry _____   great _____
   careless _____   quick _____   silent _____

Some adjectives change in a different way when they become adverbs, horrible becomes horribly.

3 Change these adjectives into adverbs.

   terrible _____   impossible _____   capable _____

Some words don't change at all, e.g. fast, almost. You can say 'a fast car' where fast is an adjective, but you can also say 'he drove fast' when fast is an adverb!

An **adjectival phrase** is a group of words which go together to make an adverb.
He packed his case as fast as he could.
As fast as he could is an adjectival phrase. It tells us how he packed his case.

4 Underline the adjectival phrases in these sentences.

(a) She spoke at the top of her voice.
(b) His fingers felt numb with cold.
(c) The holiday sounded quite exciting.
(d) He laughed rather noisily.
(e) The baby cried in a very annoying way.

Adjectival phrases can be used almost anywhere in a sentence and the sentence will still make sense. Look at this sentence:
The stars shone bright as jewels in the night sky.
Now swap it around. *Bright as jewels, the stars shone in the night sky.*
And again: *In the night sky, bright as jewels, the stars shone.*
It all depends on which way you think is best.

5 Rearrange these sentences for yourself.

(a) The sun blazed down, like a fiery ball, on the sunbathers.

(b) The girl shouted, in a very loud voice, across the room.

(c) The bell rang, loud and clear, to tell the children it was hometime.

6 On a separate piece of paper, write five more interchangeable sentences of your own.

19

Direct speech

Writing down conversations can help to make a story more interesting. To write Dotty and Milo's conversation out, remember the rules about direct speech:
- the speech marks go around the words which are actually spoken
- punctuation used by the characters goes inside the speech marks
- every time a new speaker says something, start a new line.

This is what the above conversation would look like written down:

'Hello, Dotty. What are we going to do today?' asked Milo.
'Strat wants the Gang to meet in 30 minutes.' replied Dotty.

1 Put the speech marks in the correct places in these sentences.

(a) Nina said, Is it very far to Sparkopolis from here?
(b) Hurry up, Milo. We'll be late! shouted Strat.
(c) Has anyone seen my shoes? inquired Nina, I'm sure I left them here.
(d) Dotty, pass me the book, please, asked Strat.

Once you can punctuate speech correctly, you can use more interesting words instead of **said** every time a character speaks, e.g. **shouted, inquired, asked.**

2 Here is a conversation between two characters, but it's all jumbled up. Unscramble it and write it out properly using the rules of direct speech.

Shall we go swimming? asked Nina. Oh, no! said Dotty, I haven't got a swimsuit that will fit me! Well let's go and buy a new one, laughed Nina. I would if I had any money! said Dotty sadly. I'd rather play football anyway, said Milo.

20

You can tell a lot about the way a character is feeling from how they speak and the words used to describe how they have said something. Look at these sentences.

'Hurry up!' he laughed.
'Hurry up!' she shouted impatiently.
'Hurry up!' he whispered breathlessly.
'Hurry up!' she mouthed through the window.

The spoken words are the same each time, but look how the words that follow them change the feeling of the words.

Here are some words and expressions you could use instead of said.

mumbled   whispered   stuttered
grunted   stammered   shouted
snapped   bragged   screamed
inquired   laughed   shouted angrily
cried   whinged   answered
said anxiously   whispered breathlessly   complained
said in a low voice   exclaimed

3 Use one of the above words or expressions in each of the following sentences.

(a) 'Can you see it?' he _____ .

(b) 'I told you not to do that!' she _____ .

(c) 'It was the funniest thing I ever saw!' he _____ .

(d) 'Don't let anyone see you,' she _____ .

Strat's tip
There are many more possible words you could use instead of said. Collect words when you see them in a book or hear them used and then use them in your own writing.

4 Here is a conversation between Milo and Strat. Put in a different word or expression other than 'said' each time they speak.

'Milo, have you only got one baseball cap?' _____ Strat.

'No!' _____ Milo, 'Why do you ask?'

'Well, the one you're wearing is looking a bit dirty!' _____ Strat.

'But this is my lucky hat!' _____ Milo, 'I'm not taking it off – my luck might change!'

'Well, what good luck has your hat brought you?' _____ Strat in a _____ .

'I can't think of any right now!' _____ Milo, 'Maybe you're right. It's time for a change.'

Standard English and agreeing tenses

When we are talking to friends, we sometimes say things that aren't grammatically correct, or we may use words that only people who live where we do will understand. However, when we write words down, it is important that everyone understands, so we must use what is called **Standard English**. You must also make sure that your **tenses** agree.

1 These sentences are not grammatically correct. Write them out again in Standard English so that everyone will understand.

I have did the washing up.

Should be: **I have done the washing up** or **I did the washing up.**

(a) I seen you eat that cake.

(b) I have wrote a letter to David Beckham.

(c) He drawed a really good picture.

(d) We was gonna go swimming tonight.

(e) Was you coming with us?

2 Here are some verbs in the present tense. They all change in the past tense (i.e. what has happened). Add the correct part of the verb to change present into past.

Present		Past
throw		_threw_
catch		_____
run		_____
drink	becomes	_____
eat		_____
fly		_____
write		_____

22

Double negatives should be avoided in Standard English because they use two negatives and cancel each other out. You may hear them in conversation when someone hasn't got something or when something didn't happen.

I haven't got none.

It should be: *I haven't got any.*

3 Correct these double negatives.

(a) She hadn't done nothing all day.

(b) He had never done nothing like it before.

(c) He had sweets but he never gave me none.

(d) I never wanted nothing from the shop.

4 Here is a conversation between two **characters**. They have used mixed-up tenses and double negatives. Rewrite the conversation using Standard English.

'Here, is you coming out, or what?' shouted Anya.
'Yea, I am - where are we going?' replied Tom.
'We's going to the ice rink,' said Anya.
'I've never did that before,' said Tom anxiously.
'It's easy, once you get the hang of it, but you're gonna fall over.'
'Great,' said Tom, 'but you mustn't don't laugh at me!'

Remember
- Always try to use Standard English in your writing.
- In a story, when the characters are talking to each other, it is possible to write what the characters say and not use Standard English, that is the only exception.

Apostrophes

Remember
- The apostrophe goes in the exact place where the letter or letters have been missed out.
- Apostrophes are also used to show when something belongs to someone or something.

Apostrophes show:
- where a letter or letters have been missed out to shorten a word, or join two words together, e.g. **have not** becomes **haven't**, the apostrophe goes where the 'o' in **not** used to be.
- when something belongs to someone or something, e.g. **Ravi's dog**, means the dog belongs to Ravi.

1 Change the following words using apostrophes to shorten them.

(a) I am _____   (b) They are _____   (c) He is _____
(d) You are _____   (e) We are _____   (f) You have _____

2 Now try these.

(a) did not _____   (b) have not _____   (c) will not _____
(d) would not _____   (e) could not _____   (f) had not _____
(g) who is _____   (h) she will _____   (i) let us _____

3 Rewrite the following sentences, shortening them where you can by using apostrophes. e.g. I could not eat another thing!   *I couldn't eat another thing!*

(a) I have been to Cornwall on holiday.

(b) You did not believe me, did you?

(c) She said that you could not come.

(d) He was not amused by your joke.

(e) Do not worry. We will help you.

4 Rewrite these sentences using apostrophes to show belonging.

(a) The pen of the boy.

(b) The tail of the cat.

(c) The house belonging to the Gang.

(d) The book belonging to Zeb.

(e) The sweets belonging to Milo.

(f) The nest belonging to the bird.

When things belong to more than one person, then the apostrophe goes after the 's' in the plural.
The shoes belonging to the girls. The girls' shoes.
This shows that there is more than one girl to whom the shoes belong.

5 Rewrite these sentences putting the apostrophes in the correct places.

(a) The cakes belonging to the boys.

(b) The tails belonging to the horses.

(c) The windows of the trains.

(d) The boots belonging to the footballers.

(e) The dishes belonging to the cooks.

Remember
- It is an easy mistake to make to put an apostrophe every time you write a plural, before the 's' at the end of the word, e.g. tomatoe's instead of tomatoes.
- Plurals don't need an apostrophe unless something belongs to them.
- This is a bad mistake and will cost you marks. Don't get caught out!

Planning stories

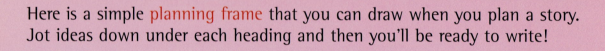

Stories can be great fun to write – whatever you can imagine can happen!

Stories always work better when you have a plan. The plan can be simple notes just to jot down your ideas.

Stories are made up of a few elements:
- characters (who's in it)
- settings (where the story takes place)
- plot (what happens)
- problems and resolutions.

Your plan should deal with each of these elements.

Here is a simple planning frame that you can draw when you plan a story. Jot ideas down under each heading and then you'll be ready to write!

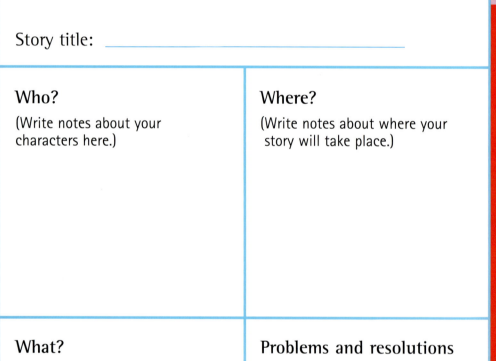

Story title: _____

Who?
(Write notes about your characters here.)

Where?
(Write notes about where your story will take place.)

What?
(Make notes about the plot here.)

Problems and resolutions
(Make notes about the interesting problems and how to get out of them.)

Strat's top tips

- Stick to no more than three main characters. Keep characters interesting and describe them well.
- Move the action of your story from one setting to another and describe your surroundings each time you move.
- Make a rough plan of your plot – think like a film director and imagine that your story is going to be made into a film. What will happen?
- Make sure that your characters have problems to face and solve as this keeps your story interesting. They can be big problems like being trapped, or small ones like forgetting a birthday present. It's how your characters deal with their problems that keeps your story moving.

Another way to plan your story is to concentrate on the plot.

Think up a way to start your story, something interesting to happen in the middle and then a brilliant way to end it!

1 Imagine you have to write a story called: My Worst Birthday. Here's a plan for this story plot.

Start: I think everyone's forgotten my birthday and I'm fed up.

Middle: I've decided to buy myself a present and go for a burger on my own.

End: When I get home there is a surprise party for me, but I feel sick because I've already had a party by myself!

Now plan these story plots.

(a) I can explain!

Start: _____

Middle: _____

End: _____

(b) The mysterious footprint in the garden

Start: _____

Middle: _____

End: _____

Remember
You don't have to put yourself in your stories; stories can be about any character. However, don't get confused about writing in the first person (I) or the third person (he, she or they). It's easy to start a story saying 'I went here, I did that' but then later in the story start writing 'she did this, he did that'. So watch out!

Beginning and ending stories

Beginning your story

The most important sentence you will write in any story is the first one. It sets the scene for the whole story, so you must take care with it and also the opening paragraph. You need to grab the reader's attention so that they want to find out what happens in your story.

You could start with:

A description – describing your surroundings in such a way that the reader wants to know more.

Dialogue – write an overheard message or conversation which gets your readers wondering.

Action – *Bang! The picture fell from the wall with a crack!*

1 Here are some ideas for stories. Write the opening sentences for each. Try to start with something different each time.

(a) You are on holiday in a caravan park in the grounds of a castle. There is a thunderstorm in the middle of the night.

_____
_____
_____
_____

(b) You find a strange book under a plant in your garden. You start to read it and find yourself becoming part of the story.

_____
_____
_____
_____

Ending your story

Your story ending should tie all the loose threads of the story together and bring everything to a conclusion. The exception is a cliffhanger, where you deliberately leave the reader not knowing what will happen. A cliffhanger does not mean you just stop writing – it has to be planned.

Try to avoid endings such as 'it was all a dream', 'I went home for tea' or 'then I went to bed' as they are boring.

2 Write your endings for the two story ideas in question 1.

(a) _____

(b) _____

3 Now try writing a whole story. Choose one of these story ideas, plan your story and then write it.

(a) **The Rescue**

Write an adventure story about a rescue. It may be you who needs to be rescued, or you may be the rescuer.

The story may take place anywhere: on a mountain, in the sea, in a castle, or even in Sparkopolis.

Explain how you came to be there. Describe your surroundings and what happens to you. Think of an interesting beginning to grab the reader's attention and an equally good ending which brings everything to a satisfying close. Choose your words carefully for maximum impact.

(b) **Mistaken Identity**

You are in your garden with a friend when a girl rushes up to the gate and says: 'Listen, I don't have much time. Here's the key. You know what to do!' Handing you a small, rusty key, she leaves as quickly as she came. You are so shocked, you call after her but she seems to have disappeared! The girl has mistaken you for someone else, but who?

Write a story about this strange adventure. What is the key for? Who did the girl think you were? What happens to you as you try to sort out the problem? How will it all end?

Remember
- Although you are not marked for your spelling in the English writing test, try to spell words correctly, because, if the examiner can't read your words, you will lose marks.
- Only use a dictionary at the end of your story, when you have finished writing, to check your spellings, if you have time. Don't waste time that could be spent on writing your ideas down.

Descriptions

Using adjectives and adverbs

Once you have the plot sorted out, the next big difference you can make to your story writing is to describe things well. To do this you will need to collect a good bank of adjectives and adverbs; write them in a notebook and use them in your stories. A thesaurus is a great place to look for interesting words.

Characters

Characters make the story come alive. You can make them distinctive by the way you describe not only their appearance, but also their feelings and their actions. It's also a good idea to have two very different characters in your story, e.g. one brave and one scared – this adds interest to see how they will cope in the situations you put them in.

1 Make a Secret Agent's dossier on one of your friends. Write something down under each category.

Name: _____
Age: _____   Height: _____
Appearance: _____
_____
_____

Likes and dislikes: _____
_____
_____

Achievements: _____
_____
_____

2 Now take all the information you have jotted down and write it up in a continuous paragraph. Read it out to your friends and see if they can guess who you have written about. (Don't read out the name of course!)

Create an atmosphere

You can really create an atmosphere by the way you describe places. Use similes to give clear descriptions and write about what you can see, hear and feel to make the reader imagine they are in the story with you.

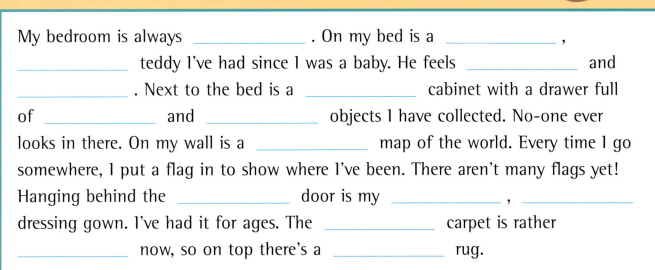

3 Here is a description of a room, with all the adjectives missed out. Choose some interesting adjectives to complete the description.

My bedroom is always _____ . On my bed is a _____ , _____ teddy I've had since I was a baby. He feels _____ and _____ . Next to the bed is a _____ cabinet with a drawer full of _____ and _____ objects I have collected. No-one ever looks in there. On my wall is a _____ map of the world. Every time I go somewhere, I put a flag in to show where I've been. There aren't many flags yet! Hanging behind the _____ door is my _____ , _____ dressing gown. I've had it for ages. The _____ carpet is rather _____ now, so on top there's a _____ rug.

4 On a separate piece of paper write a description of your own room or a place you know well.

Describe the action

When describing actions make sure you use a range of verbs and adverbs that tell us how people are doing things, e.g. **whispering quietly, barely breathing**.

5 In the next passage, put in suitable verbs or adverbs to help describe the action.

The detective crept _____ up the stairs, trying not to attract attention. _____ he stood outside the room. _____ he knocked _____ on the door. There was no answer. The detective _____ the door handle _____ and it moved. He entered the room _____ . The flat seemed to be deserted.

Experiment with verbs and adverbs until you have just the right effect.

Writing in paragraphs

Paragraphs are groups of sentences about the same subject or topic.

When you change your topic, or change your scene in a story, start a new paragraph. Paragraphs will make all the difference to your story writing and non-fiction writing because they help to organize writing into manageable parts.

When you start a new paragraph, leave a little space at the left hand side of the page before beginning to write. This is called an **indent**.

Paragraphs in story writing

Start by writing three paragraphs: the beginning, the middle and the end of your story. When you are confident about doing that, think like a film director so that every time the action or the scene changes, you start a new paragraph.

1 Rewrite this passage, organizing it into paragraphs.

> It was twelve o'clock on Monday morning and Milo was getting hungry. He had eaten his breakfast at eight, but he was hungry again. He decided to go to the shop for a sandwich. On the way there, he met Dotty, who had been buying some felt pens for her art lesson. She showed him her pens and Milo decided he would buy some of them as well. When he got home with his shopping, he found he had lost his sandwich. He must have dropped it somewhere. He would have to go back and look. On the way, he saw Zeb, who was carrying a sandwich. It looked delicious. 'Look what I've got,' said Zeb, sounding pleased. 'The man in the sandwich shop gave it to me because some silly person left it on the counter!'

Paragraphs in non-fiction writing

Paragraphs are also good for organizing non-fiction writing.

If you had to write about a particular animal, you could write one paragraph about what it looks like, another about where it lives, another about what it eats, and so on.

2 Write some short paragraphs about your family or your friends. Start a new paragraph for each person. Continue on paper if there isn't enough space here.

3 Here are some facts about some of the inhabitants of Spark Island. Write a paragraph about each group and link them with good connectives like 'on the other hand' or 'whereas' etc.

Spydrax – came from forests of Spark Island. Spider-like in appearance – like to frighten people – hyperactive – obsessed with shoes – competitive with each other about their shoes.

Spironauts – arrogant, mischievous, very noisy – like to listen to walkmans – able to tame Xybok – fly using jetpacks – wear designer shades – very short.

Letter writing

There are two kinds of letters: formal and informal. You would write formal letters to organizations like banks or to the local council, or when you don't know the person well. You would write informal letters to your friends and family.

Formal letters should be addressed correctly. Your address goes on the right-hand side of the page and the recipient's (the person to whom you are sending the letter) address and the date go on the left-hand side of the page.

3.1.03

The Hattery,
Little Chumford,
Mytown

Education Department,
Town Hall,
Mytown

Then you would start to write your letter.

1 Address letters to the following recipients. Use your own address for the sender's address.

(a) Mr. Matthews, Dodgee Car Sales, Main Road, Bigton.

(b) Mrs. S Strong, Health Centre, Nursery Road, Wellville.

Now plan the content of your letter. Here are some things to think about.

Is my letter formal or informal?
Who is going to receive it?
Where do I put the address and date?
What is the tone of my letter? (friendly, angry, complaining, sad, questioning, etc.)
What points do I want to make? - - - - -
What questions do I want to ask, or what information do I need to find out? - - - - -
Which words or expressions would be good to use?
How will I end my letter?

Now you are ready to write any kind of letter. Write real letters to newspapers, favourite pop stars and sports people. You might get a reply if your letter is interesting. You might even see your letter in the newspaper.

Persuasive writing

When you write persuasive text, you are trying to make other people see your point of view and agree with you. This means you have to present your arguments clearly and sensibly. Your choice of words is very important. You must use persuasive language.

1 Look at these two letters written to the local council asking for a new play park to be built. Which one do you think would be most successful and why?

(a)
Dear Sir,
  We need a new play park on the grass at the end of our street, because there is nothing for children to do on sunny days. My brother thinks so too. So please build one.

  Yours faithfully,
  Jim Matthews

(b)
Dear Sir,
  I am writing to ask you to consider building a new play park at the corner of Sunnybrow Road and Carlton Avenue. There are lots of children in this area and there is no safe place for them to play. I have asked the children in the area what they would like and the smaller children want swings and a slide, while the older children would like an adventure playground, a football goal and a netball/basketball post.
  The building of such a park would reduce vandalism due to boredom and allow children to exercise, which is vital for their health. It would be far less dangerous than children playing football in the road, which they are doing at present and so may reduce accidents.
  Please consider my request.
  Yours faithfully,
  Gary Bell

2 Imagine you want a play park built near your house or that your school playground needs improving. Write a persuasive letter to the council stating your demands. Remember to write good reasons for your arguments.

3 You can also persuade people by advertisements or leaflets and posters.

The people in charge of school dinners want more people to stay at school for their dinners. They are running a competition to see who can produce the best advertising slogan and information leaflet.

Start to design a poster that will persuade more children to stay for school dinners. Emphasize the healthy eating aspect of a balanced diet. Use persuasive vocabulary. Set out your work in an eye-catching and attractive way.

Words you might use:

- healthy
- nourishing
- appetizing
- home-made
- choice
- delicious
- freshly cooked
- variety
- balanced meal
- vitamins

Get ideas
- Look at advertisements in papers and magazines to get ideas for slogans and words to use.
- See how advertisers set out their posters and leaflets.

Play scripts and interviews

Play scripts are like conversations written down so that people can act them out. Extra clues, called stage directions, tell people when to enter and leave the stage. Ideas for scenery and props tell the characters how they should say a line, e.g. **in a whisper; angrily.**

1 Read this conversation.

> 'Have you got the Lixir, Strat?' 'I thought you had it, Milo!'
> 'Oh, oh, we're in real trouble now, Strat. The Elders told us to take great care of it.'
> 'Well don't panic, it can't be far. Let's retrace our steps.'

Now look at it as a playscript.

> *Scene:* a street in Sparkopolis
> Milo: Have you got the Lixir, Strat?
> Strat: (sounding worried) I thought you had it, Milo.
> Milo: (in a panicky voice) Oh, oh, we're in real trouble now, Strat. The Elders told us to take great care of it.
> Strat: (reassuringly) Well don't panic, it can't be far. Let's retrace our steps.

2 Here is another conversation. Rewrite it as a play script on a separate piece of paper. Act it out with your friends.

> *It was early evening when the Gang met at the Gang hut for a special meeting.*
> 'Okay, are we all here?' said Strat, 'let's begin the Gang meeting.'
> 'Strat, is it true that the Malvos have been seen collecting huge stocks of gooseberries from the plains around Sparkopolis and are hiding them in their houses?' inquired Nina.
> 'They must be up to something,' groaned Dotty. 'We must keep an eye on them.'
> 'Silly girls!' scoffed Milo, 'you get worried about nothing!'
> 'Do you mind?' interrupted Zeb. 'the girls are right to be worried. The Malvos seem to be up to no good and we've got to find out what they are planning.'
> 'Zeb's right,' said Strat, 'it's up to us!'
> Nina looked worried, 'We must protect Spark Island and its creatures.'
> Dotty tried to reassure her, 'Don't worry, we won't let anything happen to Spark Island.'

Interviews are a bit like play scripts, but usually only involve two people. In interviews, questions are asked to find out more about a person's character, their interests or about something special they have done. They are set out in a very similar way to play scripts, except there are no stage directions.

Remember, the more interesting the questions, the more interesting the answers. Try to think of 'open questions' where the interviewee will have to talk:

e.g. 'Did you enjoy your holiday?' is a closed question and can be answered yes or no. 'What did you most enjoy about your holiday?' is an open question and can't be answered yes or no.

3 Think up three interesting questions you would ask your favourite sportsperson or celebrity if you could interview them, followed by the answers you think the celebrities would give to each question.

Don't forget to end each question with a question mark!

Question 1: _____

Answer: _____

Question 2: _____

Answer: _____

Question 3: _____

Answer: _____

If you write your name beside 'Question 1 (2, 3)', and your interviewee's name beside 'Answer', you will have just written an interview.

4 Practise interviewing friends and family until you're really good. You could record your interviews on a cassette or computer if you have a microphone. Write your interviews down and let people read them.

Writing instructions

It is important to be able to write clearly and precisely when writing instructions. People need to know what they will need, what to do and in which order to do them so use imperative language, i.e. commands, such as: Take some card, Cut out, Mix thoroughly.

1 Look at these instructions for making a birthday card. They have been mixed up. Unscramble them and number them in the correct order. Look out for guide words like firstly, finally.

You will need a small photograph of the person whose birthday it is, 2 pieces of A4 card (one to make the window frame), foil or stick-on shapes, felt pens, scissors and a glue stick.

- [ ] Secondly, stick the photograph on to the middle of the card.

- [ ] Then draw and cut out the window frame.

- [ ] Finally, decorate with balloons and stars cut out of foil or with sticky shapes.

- [ ] After you have attached the frame, use felt tip pens to write Happy Birthday on the front.

- [ ] Now stick the window frame over the photograph.

- [ ] Firstly, fold a piece of A4 card in half.

Instructions like recipes and craft ideas usually list the items you need before the instructions so that you can collect everything. There are often pictures or diagrams to help. The instructions are often numbered or written in bullet points rather than paragraphs to make it clear.

2 Give directions to your parents or a friend to a place that you both know. Use words like: take the first right; go straight on; turn left.

Here is a frame to help you plan your instructional writing.

Remember to mention landmarks that might help.

Purpose (What do I want people to be able to do or understand from my instructions?)	
Audience (This will affect the language you use. Are the instructions for a young child, a class-mate, an adult?)	
Ingredients or resources (Will I need to make a list of things people might need before they start to follow my instructions?)	
Special language (Remember to use imperative language, e.g. Take a sheet of paper; fold the right edge. You are telling someone what to do and how to do it so use the correct words and expressions.)	
Step-by-step (Break down the instructions into steps.) • • • • •	
Ending (Make sure the instructions have a clear ending.)	

Get ideas
Read the instructions for games and recipes to see the kind of language used and how they are set out.

3 Write out the instructions for, and illustrate, your favourite recipe or an easy craft idea. Then give it to your friend or parent and see if it is clear enough for them to follow.

Journalistic and leaflet writing

You may be asked to design posters or leaflets, write newspaper or magazine articles or write lists or instructions. All these different kinds of non-fiction texts, still need to be planned. This is to make sure that the information has been put down in the best possible way.

Things to think about
- What is the purpose of my writing? (to inform, to persuade, a report etc.)
- Who is my writing aimed at? (children, adults)
- How shall I organize my writing? (in paragraphs, bullet points, a list)
- What information do I need to get across?
- What are my key points?
- Will I be using sub-headings? What will they be?
- Can I think of special words and phrases I might use?
- How will I end my piece?

Last week, Zeb had to write an article about Xybok for the Sparkopolis newspaper. He had to think about all the information he wanted to put down before he started to write. Here is his plan.

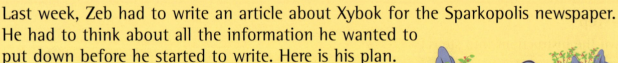

- What is the purpose of my writing?
  My writing is to inform people.
- Who is my writing aimed at?
  Children aged about 9-11.
- How shall I organize my writing?
  In paragraphs.
- What information do I need to get across?
  What Xybok look like; what they eat; how big they are; where they live; if they are dangerous or not; how to look after them.
- What are my key points?
  Xybok are large; they like to graze; they eat raspberries and gooseberries; they are friendly; they live on the plains around Sparkopolis; they can move quickly and take part in races with Spironauts as jockeys.
- Will I be using sub-headings? What will they be?
  I will use a new paragraph for each new aspect of the Xybok.
- Can I think of special words and phrases I might use?
  docile, grazing, friendly, herbivores, shy, surprisingly gentle
- How will I end my piece?
  A sentence summing up all the qualities of the Xybok.

1 Here are two ideas for you to plan and then write. Remember, depending on the kind of writing it is, you won't always need to put something down under every single heading on the plan. Work on a separate piece of paper if there isn't enough space here.

(a) Write a magazine article about your favourite pop star/group or sports person. Find out information by reading books, or use what you already know. Think about how you will set it out to be interesting. You might want to add a photo or illustration!

(b) Design a leaflet for a new leisure centre that is opening in your town. Write about all the things you can do there; don't forget prices and opening times!

Planning frame
Title of writing:
Purpose:
Audience:
Organization:
Information/key points:
Sub-headings:
Special words and phrases:
Ending:

I read lots of newspapers and magazines. It helps me to be a better writer.

Glossary

adjective	a word which is added to a noun to describe it, e.g. green, beautiful.
adverb	a word which is added to a verb to describe it or modify it, e.g. slowly, happily.
apostrophe	a punctuation mark. It is either used to indicate where a word has been shortened and a letter or letters have been missed out, e.g. I am – I'm; have not – haven't. Or it can be used to show possession when something belongs to someone or something, e.g. Jane's book, Bill's pen.
character	an individual featured in a poem, story or play.
clause	a distinct part of a sentence including a verb. In a main clause it makes sense on its own, e.g. I'll tell you. In a subordinate clause it gives more information about the main clause, e.g. I'll tell you when I get home.
colon (:)	a punctuation mark which introduces a list or a second clause connected to the first: e.g. you will need: or He was happy: he had just won the Lottery!
comma (,)	a punctuation mark used to separate items in a list, or to separate parts of a sentence.
conjunction	a word used to link sentences or clauses, e.g. because, but, so.
connective	words or phrases used to link different parts of text, e.g. some time later.
dialogue	a conversation between two characters.
double negative	the use of two negatives which cancel each other out, e.g. 'I haven't done nothing' should be 'I haven't done anything' or 'I have done nothing'.
metaphor	used to write about something as if it really was something else, e.g. the sun was a big orange in a blue bowl.
noun	a naming word for people, places and things.
paragraph	a section of a piece of writing, marking change of focus, place, time or speaker.
persuasive text	text which tries to make the reader agree with the writer's point of view; a way to present effective arguments.
phrase	two or more words which act as one unit, e.g. a green car; as soon as possible.
planning frame	prompts and suggestions to help plan different forms of writing.
plural	more than one of something: tigers, lions, apples.
semi-colon (;)	a punctuation mark used to separate phrases or clauses in a sentence.
simile	a way of describing things by comparing them to other things, e.g. as bright as the sun; soft, like a newly-washed jumper.
Standard English	a way of writing English which has been formalised and agreed so that it can be widely understood (without slang or dialect).
tense	indicates that something is happening; in the past, present, future, or if it might happen (conditional tense).
thesaurus	a book which groups words of similar meaning together.
verb	a doing or being word, e.g. playing, running, were.

Answers

Starting and ending sentences

1. Monday 14th October
Today has been very good. I played a trick on Zeb by hiding his favourite book. He was looking all over for it. Nina tried to help him. They even went to the library in Sparkopolis and searched every part of Sparkley Square. I had to tell them the truth eventually and they were mad. Zeb even thought the Xybok had eaten it by mistake, thinking its red cover was a giant raspberry. I laughed for ages. Now I need to think up a new trick for Tuesday.

2. Proper nouns: Tuesday, Brighton, Fifi, England, Strat, River Thames
Common nouns: cat, school, hedge, book, raspberry, fork

3. (a) Are you coming swimming today?
   (b) Stop that now!
   (c) Sparkopolis is a big city.
   (d) Statements must end with a full stop.
   (e) Are you going to eat all that cake yourself?
   (f) Leave him alone!
   (g) Dotty is a dreamer, isn't she?
   (h) It was absolutely fantastic!
   (i) Have you got any homework tonight?
   (j) I wonder how many sentences I've got right.

4. There are 4 question marks and 3 exclamation marks.

Connectives and conjunctives

1. (a) Nina was miserable because nobody wanted to go out.
   (b) Strat is popular so he is the leader of the Gang.
   (c) Dotty went to the library, then she went to Spark Park.
   (d) Zeb likes reference books because he likes to collect facts.
   (Other words would fit)

3. (a) Spark Island is a fun place; consequently people like living there.
   (b) Crombies are very studious people, although they are friendly.
   (c) Milo can be sensible, although he often sulks.
   (d) Crombies are very quiet, however Spironauts are definitely not!

4. (a) Soon after/In less than a second
   (b) Meanwhile
   (c) A few years later
   (d) In less than a second

5. (a) First, take two slices of bread ...
   (b) Secondly, slice or grate the cheese ...
   (c) Then, arrange the cheese ...
   (d) After that, add pickle or ...
   (e) Finally, put the other slice ...

Commas and colons

1. (a) The Elders needed Lixir, unicycles, raspberries and books.
   (b) Nina tidied out her bag. She found sweets, a book, a map of Sparkopolis, a pencil and a button from her coat.
   (c) To get to the park go straight along Blackmore Road, turn right, then left and cross over by the library.
   (d) To make the model you will need card, glue, thin string, pens, scissors, a paper fastener and a lot of patience!
   (e) The library is open on Monday, Tuesday, Wednesday and Friday.

2 and 3 Check to see that your child has added commas appropriately to his or her lists.

4 and 5 Similarly, check to see that your child has preceded his or her list with a colon and separated the items with commas.

Clauses

1. (a) Strat was bored, but he knew an adventure wasn't far away.
   (b) Everyone laughed, although poor Milo got soaking wet.

(c) The diver explored the sea bed, even though there were sharks nearby.

(d) You can't go out, unless you tidy your room first.

2 (a) even though

(b) especially since

(c) because

(d) while

4 (a) Nina, who is a friendly girl, rarely loses her temper.

(b) While visiting the zoo Milo, who was the youngest of the Gang, got lost.

(c) Sparkopolis, which is a large city, was designed by the Elders.

(d) Strat hoped, as he unlocked the box, he would find the treasure.

5 (a) Strat, after being hit by the ball, had a sore eye.

(b) Nina, because she was being chased by a bull, jumped over the hedge.

(c) Milo, who is the youngest, can be mischievous.

Semi-colons and brackets

1 (a) It was nearly midnight; everyone had gone to bed.

(b) Your book looks interesting; mine is a mystery story.

(c) I keep my stickers in this album; I keep my photos in this box.

(d) My favourite colour is red; I think you prefer blue.

2 It was a winter's night; cold and dark. In the trees, owls hooted overhead; on the forest floor, small creatures scampered through leaves. Strat was glad of his torch; it had been a present from Nina. Everywhere he moved, eyes seemed to follow him; huge, staring eyes. Strat shivered and pulled his coat around him. He couldn't give up now; he had to go on.

4 (a) The Elders (although wise) were incredibly forgetful.

(b) The Phliplids were rebuilding their (so far invisible) spaceship.

(c) The Malvos denied upsetting the Crombies (as they always do) but the Crombies were convinced of their guilt.

(d) Milo had borrowed Zeb's encyclopedia (without permission) and now had raspberry jam all over the cover.

Adjectives

1 As long as the choice of adjective is appropriate, the answer is correct.

2 (a) I couldn't wait to eat the sweet orange.

(b) The old castle walls felt rough and damp.

(c) The stormy sea sent waves of salty water over the harbour.

(d) The beautiful scent of flowers filled the small room.

3 Your child's choice of adjectives - whatever is appropriate.

4 Again, your child's choice of adjectives from the list.

5 (a) He was the most awful footballer I have ever seen.

(b) She was the least shy person in the room.

(c) She was the loudest singer in the group.

(d) He had one older brother and two younger sisters.

Similes and metaphors

1 The castle stood like a grey giant on the top of the hill. Its battlements were like dragon's teeth and flags flew from each turret like washing on a line. The huge, strong door loomed up in front of us as big as an elephant and we knocked as timidly as mice. From behind the door, a sound like thunder echoed across the flagstones. Someone was approaching!

Adverbs

1. (a) Strat crept **silently** through the pirates' caves.
   (b) Milo dreamed **happily** of getting a new baseball cap.
   (c) Zeb read the instructions **carefully** before trying the experiment.
   (d) Dotty rode her bike **quickly** down the road.
   (e) Nina spoke **excitedly** about her adventures.

2. badly, merrily, greatly, carelessly, quickly, silently

3. terribly, impossibly, capably

4. (a) She spoke **at the top of her voice**.
   (b) His fingers felt **numb with cold**.
   (c) The holiday sounded **quite exciting**.
   (d) He laughed **rather noisily**.
   (e) The baby cried **in a very annoying way**.

5. (a) The sun blazed down, on the sunbathers, like a fiery ball. *or*
   Like a fiery ball, the sun blazed down on the sunbathers. *or*
   Like a fiery ball, on the sunbathers, the sun blazed down.
   (b) The girl shouted, across the room, in a very loud voice. *or*
   In a very loud voice, across the room, the girl shouted. *or*
   Across the room, the girl shouted, in a very loud voice. *or*
   Across the room, in a very loud voice, the girl shouted.
   (c) The bell rang, to tell the children it was hometime, loud and clear. *or*
   Loud and clear, the bell rang, to tell the children it was hometime. *or*
   Loud and clear, to tell the children it was hometime, the bell rang. *or*
   To tell the children it was hometime, the bell rang, loud and clear.

Direct speech

1. (a) Nina said, 'Is it very far to Sparkopolis from here?'
   (b) 'Hurry up, Milo. We'll be late!' shouted Strat.
   (c) 'Has anyone seen my shoes?' inquired Nina, 'I'm sure I left them here.'
   (d) 'Dotty, pass me the book please,' asked Strat.

2. 'Shall we go swimming?' asked Nina.
   'Oh, no!' said Dotty, 'I haven't got a swimsuit that will fit me!'
   'Well let's go and buy a new one,' laughed Nina.
   'I would if I had any money!' said Dotty sadly.
   'I'd rather play football anyway,' said Milo.
   (Each new speaker should also start a new line.)

3. Your child's choice from the selection offered.

4. As long as the choice is appropriate, mark as correct.

Standard English and agreeing tenses

1. (a) I saw you eat that cake.
   (b) I have written a letter to David Beckham. *or* I wrote a letter to David Beckham.
   (c) He drew a really good picture.
   (d) We were going to go swimming tonight.
   (e) Were you coming with us? *or* Were you going to come with us?

2. catch - caught, run - ran, drink - drank, eat - ate, fly - flew, write - wrote

3. (a) She hadn't done anything all day. *or* She had done nothing all day.
   (b) He had never done anything like it before. *or* He had done nothing like it before.
   (c) He had sweets but didn't give me any. *or* He had sweets but never gave any to me.
   (d) I wanted nothing from the shop. *or* I didn't want anything from the shop.

4. 'Here, are you coming out, or not?' shouted Anya.
   'Yes, I am - where are we going?' replied Tom.
   'We are going to the ice rink,' said Anya.
   'I've never done that before,' said Tom anxiously.
   'It's easy, once you get the hang of it (*or* learn how to do it), but you are going to fall over.'
   'Great,' said Tom, 'but you mustn't laugh at me!'

47

Apostrophes

1. (a) I am – I'm (b) They are – they're (c) He is – he's (d) You are – you're (e) We are – we're (f) You have – you've

2. (a) did not – didn't (b) have not – haven't (c) will not – won't (d) would not – wouldn't (e) could not – couldn't (f) had not – hadn't (g) who is – who's (h) she will – she'll (i) let us – let's.

3. (a) I've been to Cornwall on holiday.
   (b) You didn't believe me, did you?
   (c) She said that you couldn't come.
   (d) He wasn't amused by your joke.
   (e) Don't worry. We'll help you.

4. (a) The boy's pen. (b) The cat's tail. (c) The Gang's house. (d) Zeb's book. (e) Milo's sweets. (f) The bird's nest.

5. (a) The boys' cakes. (b) The horses' tails. (c) The trains' windows. (d) The footballers' boots. (e) The cooks' dishes.

Writing in paragraphs

It was twelve o'clock on Monday morning and Milo was getting hungry. He had eaten his breakfast at eight, but he was hungry again. He decided to go to the shop for a sandwich.

On the way there, he met Dotty, who had been buying some felt pens for her art lesson. She showed him her pens and Milo decided he would buy some of them as well.

When he got home with his shopping, he found he had lost his sandwich. He must have dropped it somewhere. He would have to go back and look.

On the way, he saw Zeb, who was carrying a sandwich. It looked delicious.
'Look what I've got,' said Zeb, sounding pleased. 'The man in the sandwich shop gave it to me because some silly person left it on the counter!'

Play scripts and interviews

Scene: The Gang hut

Strat: Okay, are we all here? Let's begin the Gang meeting.

Nina: (inquiringly) Is it true that the Malvos have been seen collecting huge stocks of gooseberries from the plains around Sparkopolis and are hiding them in their houses?

Dotty: (groaning) They must be up to something. We must keep an eye on them.

Milo: (in a scoffing manner) Silly girls! You get worried about nothing!

Zeb: (interrupting) Do you mind, the girls are right to be worried. The Malvos seem to be up to no good and we've got to find out what they are planning.

Strat: Zeb's right – it's up to us!

Nina: (looking worried) We must protect Spark Island and its creatures.

Dotty: (reassuringly) Don't worry, we won't let anything happen to Spark Island.

Writing instructions

1. Firstly, fold a piece of A4 card in half.
2. Secondly, stick the photograph on to the middle of the card.
3. Then draw and cut out the window frame.
4. Now stick the window frame over the photograph.
5. After you have attached the frame, use felt tip pens to write Happy Birthday on the front.
6. Finally, decorate with balloons and stars cut out of foil, or with sticky shapes.